Messy Church® is grow  who have never set fo. .... enjoying Messy Church, and every month more Messy Churches are started all over the UK and worldwide. Messy Church is proving effective in sharing God's good news with families across denominations and church traditions. We estimate that some 100,000 people belong to Messy Churches—and the number is growing all the time. For more information about Messy Church, visit www.messychurch.org.uk.

Messy Church is enabled, resourced and supported by BRF (Bible Reading Fellowship), a Registered Charity, as one of its core ministries. BRF makes Messy Church freely available and derives no direct income from the work that we do to support it in the UK and abroad.

Would you be willing to support this ministry with your prayer and your giving? To find out more, please visit www.messychurch.org.uk/champions.

Messy Church® is a registered word mark and the logo is a registered device mark of
The Bible Reading Fellowship
Text copyright © Lucy Moore and Jane Leadbetter 2012
The author asserts the moral right
to be identified as the author of this work

Published by
The Bible Reading Fellowship
15 The Chambers, Vineyard
Abingdon OX14 3FE
United Kingdom
Tel: +44 (0)1865 319700
Email: enquiries@brf.org.uk
Website: www.brf.org.uk
BRF is a Registered Charity

ISBN 978 0 85746 050 9
First published 2012
10 9 8 7 6 5 4 3 2 1 0
All rights reserved

Acknowledgments
Page 33: Scripture quotation taken from the Holy Bible, New International Version,
copyright © 1973, 1978, 1984 by International Bible Society, used by permission of
Hodder & Stoughton Publishers, a member of the Hachette Livre Group UK.
All rights reserved. 'NIV' is a registered trademark of International Bible Society.
UK trademark number 1448790.

A catalogue record for this book is available from the British Library

Printed in Singapore by Craft Print International Ltd

The paper used in the production of this publication was supplied
by mills that source their raw materials from sustainably managed forests.
Soy-based inks were used in its printing and the laminate film is biodegradable.

Starting your Messy CHURCH

A beginner's guide for churches

Lucy Moore and Jane Leadbetter

For Lesley Baker and Denise Williams, two friends who started the first Messy Church, who have stuck with it right from the beginning, who have thrown ideas into (and, mercifully, out of) more planning meetings than any of us can remember and who help our Messy Church become what God wants it to be through their tireless love, faith, wisdom and hope.
LM

For Sandra McCann and Christine Eyre at L19: Messy Church for their creativity and vision for the local community, and for the best bacon butties ever!
JL

Contents

Introduction

If you're wondering about starting a Messy Church, this book is for you. It's short, punchy and easily passed round a team who may not have time to read the longer Messy Church books or watch the DVD. It gets the basics across quickly and will give you a good idea of whether or not Messy Church is for you. It sets out clearly just what you'll need to consider and will also help you avoid some of the pitfalls other teams have encountered on their Messy Church journeys.

Combined with the downloadable material on the Messy Church website, you should now have all the help you need to get going with a Messy Church in your community, but don't forget that even more help will come from other people. Your neighbouring Messy Churches will be delighted to cheer you on and share their experiences. The network of Regional Coordinators grows each year and you'll find expert help and news of local events from the one nearest you (contact details on the website). You can also contact the BRF Messy Church team via the website, so you need never be alone with a problem to solve or a wonderful story that you simply have to share with someone.

God has graciously and inexplicably chosen to work through many Messy Churches, drawing together teams of Christians who have suddenly found the opportunity through it to share his story and their own story of faith in a non-threatening way, and drawing in families with no church connection to show them how warm, welcoming, relevant and fun a church can be. This may be for you too. Our prayer is that every Messy Church will be an opportunity for congregations and teams to meet Father, Son and Holy Spirit, and a place where the kingdom of heaven has the space to grow within individuals and families to the glory of God and for the healing and wholeness of the local community.

Lucy Moore and Jane Leadbetter

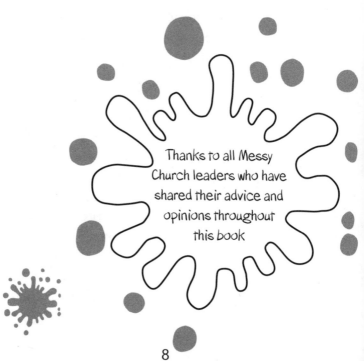

Thanks to all Messy Church leaders who have shared their advice and opinions throughout this book

Messy Church:
the bigger picture

Before you leap into a morass of glue and spaghetti, ask yourself a question:

Why are you thinking about starting a Messy Church?

There may be any number of honest answers, but what matters is that you want to help families meet Jesus. With that in place you can't go far wrong, whatever you do.

I love the idea of Messy Church. This is what we need. I suppose we just need to get on with it

Possibly good reasons for starting a Messy Church

- We want to make disciples.
- The people in our area who don't belong to church would like coming to a Messy Church.
- We want to share the love of God in Jesus in a way that's as accessible as possible to families.
- We believe that the best way for people of all ages to come closer to God is by journeying together.
- We want to share Jesus more than we want to share our particular denominational traditions.
- We want to model who Jesus is to those around us.
- We believe God is in Messy Church and we want to follow where he leads.
- We think Jesus is the person to give people in our community life in all its fullness.
- And many more. (In fact, *many* more good reasons than bad ones, we find, as we hear people getting excited at Messy Church training events. Which is reassuring.)

Possibly less good reasons for starting a Messy Church

- It's the latest thing so it must be good.
- The church up the road is running a Messy Church so we need to or we'll get left out.
- The minister says we need one.
- We need younger people in our church to do the jobs we used to do when we were young.
- We want to revamp our Sunday congregation.
- We want to get together for a nice sociable time with knitting and paint.
- It sounds fun.
- We're bored with sermons and want a change.
- I have a stationery fetish that I can indulge shamelessly.

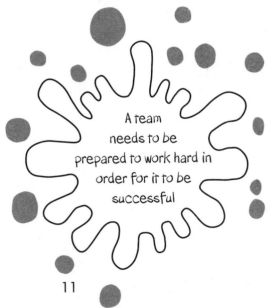

A team needs to be prepared to work hard in order for it to be successful

Running a Messy Church is hard work, tiring, relentless, may make you vulnerable to deep disappointment and hurt, and may bring you into conflict with people who don't get it or who take you for a ride. (Sounds like the experience of Jesus already.) It will bring you into a greater intimacy with heaps of raw sausages than you really want. It will make you search your soul for answers to questions you've never thought about or cared about before. It will send you into a panic about your own Christian journey and how you articulate and live out that story. And it will be exhilarating, eye-opening, moving, radical and might/will/should change the way you look at Christ and his church. We thoroughly recommend it.

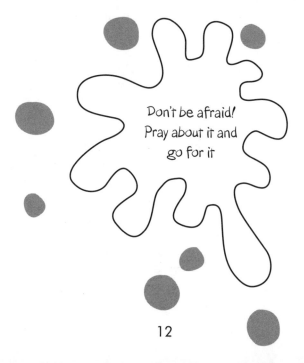

Don't be afraid!
Pray about it and
go for it

All this is to say that starting a Messy Church is about involving you and your team and community in something bigger than 'a little kraft klub for the kiddies'. You are being a pioneer, taking on the role of a church leader, whether you're ordained or not: this is serious stuff and not to be undertaken lightly or without due reverence, as the Marriage Service says. But it's also a huge amount of fun and adventure: just save yourselves a lot of grief by deciding right from the start that you are all in the business of making disciples. The way you go about making disciples may involve horrifying amounts of icing sugar and glitter glue, but it's always there, this priority that will keep you all going through the hard times: we're here to make disciples, not to try to get people coming to our church service or to give them a Nice Time. It's like an artist imagining the whole picture in her head before she knuckles down and starts painting in the detail of the clouds in the top left-hand corner: she knows in the broadest terms what the big picture will be, even if it changes hugely in the process. Messy Church, like other forms of church, traditional or new, is ultimately about making disciples.

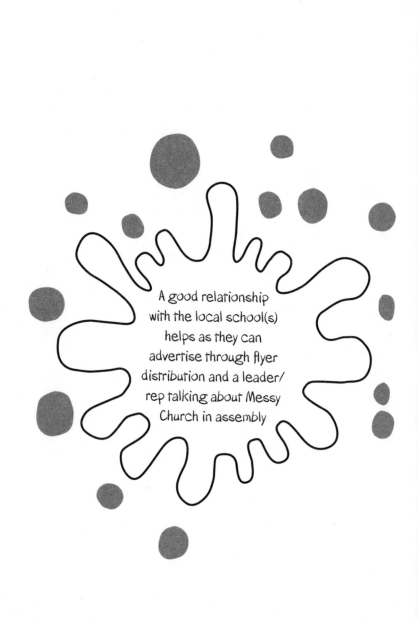

A good relationship with the local school(s) helps as they can advertise through flyer distribution and a leader/rep talking about Messy Church in assembly

What Messy Church is and isn't

All this is explored in depth in *Messy Church*, the first book. But as you have taken the trouble to buy this one, here's a brief recap: it's a form of church for children and adults that involves creativity, celebration and hospitality. It meets at a time (and sometimes in a place) that suits people who don't already belong to church and usually looks something like this: welcome, craft time, celebration or 'overt' worship, meal. Most meet once a month, though a few are more frequent or more occasional.

In the words of Claire Dalpra of The Sheffield Centre: 'Messy Church is an all-age fresh expression of church that offers counter-cultural transformation of family life through families coming together to be, to make, to eat and to celebrate God.'

It's not a children's church.

It's not a way of attracting more people to your existing Sunday services, though this might happen.

It's a church for people at all stages of their faith journey and of any age, a congregation that is as valuable and worthy of investment as any of your other congregations.

Children are an integral part of the congregation and are both models of discipleship and disciples themselves, as are the adults who play the same dual roles. You'll see an experienced Christian learning from a less experienced one and vice versa; a child teaching an adult; sometimes one family learns from another en masse; sometimes the Christian community demonstrates how to live for Jesus to those who don't yet know him; sometimes a parent teaches a child something.

If discipleship needs a mixture of formal learning, informal learning and social learning, Messy Church has elements of all three as it (formally) explores the Bible through activities and story, provides opportunities for informal conversation and observation, and encourages all sorts of levels of social learning both at the gathered Messy Church and in encouragement to take that learned faith back into the home during the rest of the month. Of the three sorts of learning, it is stronger on the social and informal ways of learning.

How it all began

Messy Church began in the Anglican church of St Wilfrid's in Cowplain, a suburb of Portsmouth. As Lucy was on the core team of this first Messy Church and was also working for BRF's ministry among children, BRF was the logical place to base the wider ministry of Messy Church as it developed in training, website and publications, giving the movement the backing of a larger infrastructure than St Wilf's could have provided.

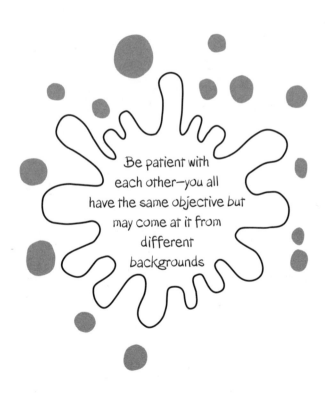

Be patient with each other—you all have the same objective but may come at it from different backgrounds

It will take time.
Don't expect to share
this one meeting and have it all
running a month later.
It may take six months

Why the shape?

The welcome

The welcome time comes from an understanding that the people who come to a Messy Church often don't come into a church easily; they need an encouraging warm welcome. An after-school Messy Church may need a longer welcome time than a weekend one, as arrivals from different schools mean a very staggered starting time, whereas at the weekend, most people can arrange to arrive at around the same time. An unstructured time of conversation, colouring, chilling, chatting with drinks and snacks can be a relief after a structured day.

The craft time

The craft time gives an hour for leisurely unhurried experimentation and enjoyment of the various crafts on offer. The number of crafts varies, but may be between five and ten, enough to allow plenty to fill the time but not so many that people feel overwhelmed by choice. They are all themed around the Bible theme of the day and may well come at the subject tangentially or obliquely, but are no less valuable for that. There is a variety of activities to appeal to both genders and all ages and learning styles.

The celebration

The celebration makes the theme overt and articulates some of the learning, placing it in the context of worship rather than cerebral knowledge alone. It is a celebration of God, of his redeeming work in Jesus, of our lives and identity in his story, of our community life and identity as well as our family and individual lives.

The meal

The meal feeds body and soul as the congregation sits round tables or picnic rugs as equals and breaks bread (or pasta or jacket potatoes) together in a non-verbal expression of the feast of the kingdom of heaven, where all are accepted and everyone belongs without a need to earn their place or fight for recognition and status.

Each of these elements of Messy Church provides opportunities to build relationships and show who God is in words and actions.

Why the values?

Creativity is about reflecting who God is as creator of new things and re-creator of people and communities who are broken. It comes across most strongly in the craft time but bubbles up in the imaginative approach to dealing with problems and opportunities as they arise and refusing to be hide-bound in any aspect of Messy Church.

Celebration is about the joy of being a child of God and a member of this marvellous body we call the church. It's about saying yes, there is a huge amount to celebrate in our faith life, even if the world around us is falling apart. It's also about celebrating in the sense of 'marking' or 'recognising as significant' each person, each family, the church community and the God we serve.

Hospitality waves the flag for the Christ who welcomes the people on the edges of society, who makes them his priority and his joy. It means shaping what we do around the needs of those who are marginalised, and being ready to be changed by them. It's about welcome and food and grace and giving.

Christ-centred means that although a gathering like this could easily be a happy time if we removed the church element completely and ran it on the theme of The Seaside or Jungles, what we want to do is bring people closer to Jesus Christ.

All-age means that Messy Church is not just for children but has something for everyone and that the fact of having all ages present knocking up against each other in the same room and doing the same activities is important to us. It's a recognition that it is a gift from God to be family across the generations, whether by blood ties or faith ties.

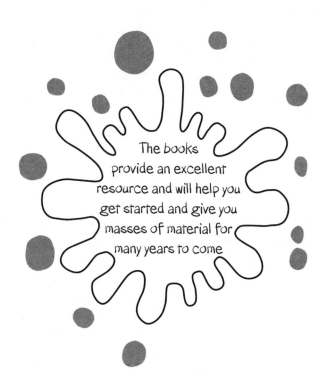

The books provide an excellent resource and will help you get started and give you masses of material for many years to come

Commitment needed to start and run a Messy Church

Prayer

As soon as you start thinking about starting a Messy Church, start praying and encourage others to pray too.

Wholeheartedness

Janet Tredrea from Cornwall writes of her wide experience of Messy Churches:

I can think of one (rural church) which has needed an injection of new life in which all the members can take part. The idea of Messy Church was put to the remaining members (numbers depleted recently as several left the congregation because of disillusionment and lack of vision) as a last ditch attempt to promote the gospel to outsiders. It was stressed that everyone had to take ownership—the elderly could pray, give donations of food or money and all the able bodied were to join the 'hands-on team'. It worked—the Spirit was fanned back into more prominent life, team spirit is vibrant, fellowship is had every month in studying the topic of the next session and that dying church now has an active 'wing' to which the outside community is sitting up and taking notice and enthusiastically supporting. The disillusioned are back on the team and the dying church has been 'resurrected'!

This story illustrates the power of having a whole church committed to a Messy Church and the 'payback' for insisting on an all-or-nothing approach. Churches work in different ways and what was right for this church may be wrong for another, where the Messy Church might be overpowered if every member of the inherited church was committed to serving on the team.

Frequency

Most Messy Churches operate monthly. This is still a considerable commitment when so many aspects of this style of church have to be pulled together for the messy two hours. But being monthly rather than weekly has the advantage that it gives time for preparation, reflection and making changes between one month and the next. Many team members find it easier to commit to a monthly session than to a weekly one, and many messy congregation members find the same in their busy lives. So far, most anecdotal evidence points to Messy Churches that attempt to be weekly (for very good reasons) tending to suffer burnout after two years or so, though there are honourable exceptions.

Team

Many Messy Churches operate very well with a small core team and a larger 'turn up on the day' team. It hardly needs saying that the more envisioned and committed each individual is the more effective your Messy Church is likely to be in its mission. This dedication might come further down the line and you may find the team grow in excitement and commitment as they see God at work, rather than coming to the first Messy Church with all guns blazing. You may or may not want to read that leaders say repeatedly that they're glad they didn't know when they started how tiring it would be!

Support

The minister and leadership team of the church is a crucial body to have onside. If you don't have their support, you should seriously consider whether the idea is the right way forward, or if it's going to work or have any longevity. It could provoke division and competition if it is not supported at all levels of your church.

Money

Some Messy Churches charge a small entrance fee; some provide everything for free; some have donation pots, pigs or buckets. A contribution from your 'sending church' is a gesture of commitment and will ease the way as you discover what you are likely to need to budget every month. If people protest, either explain the missional aspect of what you're planning or check what the flower budget is each month.

Space

A church building has advantages: it may be superficially rent-free, be associated with the historical Christian presence in the area, have storage space and have been prayed in for centuries. But it may be cold, dangerous, inhospitable and kitchen- or toilet-free. Schools, pubs, community halls and village halls are all alternatives.

Work together?

Many Messy Churches work brilliantly where two or three churches have joined together to run one joint Messy Church: is this an option for you?

The wider network

If you set up your Messy Church in a vacuum relating to nobody else, you may be missing out and others cannot benefit from your experience. Joining a local, a denominational or the whole international Messy network is one step you can take to help sustain you and the team in days ahead which may be tougher if the initial pioneering spirit wears off and tiredness sets in. You can be in touch with your Regional Coordinator, and sign up to the newsletter and Directory on the website to stay in touch.

CRB checks

The best thing is to talk to your Child Protection Officer or the representative who deals with safe-guarding vulnerable adults. Each denomination and area has different rules for this form of church where children are present but are the responsibility of an adult rather than of the church. Some basic good-practice guidelines should be distributed to and discussed with team members.

Other certification

The Basic Food Hygiene qualification is advisable for the kitchen staff. A First Aid qualification is also a good idea.

We're in need of this if our families in the community are to be introduced to Jesus

Checklist of starting strategies

- Listen to God.
- Listen to people outside church.
- Communicate with people in church.

The rest is detail, but it may help to...

- Pray.
- Pray some more with other people.
- Think imaginatively about your area and listen to people who don't go to church or who are on the edge of church to find out what the real needs are from their point of view. You will find helpful pointers to get you going with listening to your community on the Fresh Expressions website www.sharetheguide.org. Watch the first two tracks of the Messy Church DVD and pass it around your possible core team or have a popcorn night and watch the two tracks together and discuss whether it will work for you.
- Talk to your church leaders, listen to them and pray with them.

- Visit a Messy Church near you and ask as many questions as they have patience to answer. Ask questions of the team, the congregation and the main leaders (see suggested questions below, page 41).

- Pray some more and listen some more. The more sure you are that this is a calling from God, not a flash in the pan, the easier it will be later on if things get tough.

- Talk to lots of people in your church (especially the unlikely people) to get them engaged and possibly prepared to pray/cook/be crafty/clean up and so on. Get everyone excited! Look for people on the edge who have never been asked to help before. Ask people to do discrete jobs rather than everything.

- Plan a budget and investigate sources of funding.

- Get the go-ahead from your church leadership team (this should also ensure you are insured under your church's policy). There is a suggested introductory session in the Messy Church DVD to bring the idea to life and share the vision.

- Write a clear list of your aims (a suggested starting point is included below) and give them to your whole team.

- Get everyone CRB checked who needs to be, and clear about best practice as regards children and vulnerable adults, somebody qualified with Basic Food Hygiene, a First Aider and anything else your church requires you to have qualifications-wise.
- Get together a small planning team and get praying and plotting your first Messy Church in detail.

Aims of Messy Church in...

- To provide an opportunity for people of all ages to worship together.
- To help people of all ages feel they belong in church and to each other.
- To help people have fun and be creative together.
- To introduce Jesus through hospitality, friendship, stories and worship.
- ?
- ?
- ?

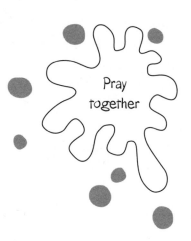

Pray together

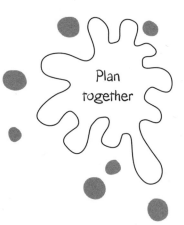

Plan together

Why the network?

How about a local Messy Church get-together of leaders of all the groups in the Diocese to discuss progress, successes, problems, etc.? We would like to know how to stop it becoming too popular as we are just about at capacity and still growing!

(Email from a Messy Church leader
in Hampshire)

Interesting point 1

Many Messy Churches are run by women, and women in general are good at sharing both ignorance and knowledge.

Interesting point 2

God sets the lonely in families (Psalm 68:8).

Interesting point 3

In our discussions about long-term sustainability of fresh expressions, the need to be linked into a wider network than just the local fresh expression is proving to be hugely important a few years after starting.

You may not have the time or energy to link into any Messy Church networks when you are in the throes of starting up your own Messy Church. But it is a question to look at reasonably soon as the benefits can be enormous.

Messy Fiestas are training days to introduce the idea of Messy Church and to give people a chance to air reservations and hear stories of what really happens. They are advertised on the Messy Church website and are a great opportunity to meet other people at a similar stage.

Messy e-news: BRF sends out a monthly newsletter free of charge to anyone who signs up for it. This is a good way of staying in touch with what others are doing in Messy Church and of staying aware of new projects that may resource your own Messy Church.

Regional Coordinators are volunteers across the UK and overseas who are passionate about Messy Church, are in close touch with BRF's Messy Church Team and want to help people in their region to do it as well as possible. The list is on the website.

Messy blog: the Messy blog on the website is a useful trickle of developments and stories from across the world.

The Messy Church website puts you straight through to the BRF Messy Church Team for enquiries or comments or to share stories. We're very accessible and will reply as soon as we possibly can, events and travel permitting. You'll also find here a growing number of resources and ideas that other Messy Churches have generously contributed.

Visiting a local Messy Church: the Directory provides many contact details for existing Messy Churches and there may be some near you. As we've said, a very valuable step in starting up is to visit somebody else's Messy Church and learn from their experiences, both good and bad. (See the section on visiting a Messy Church on page 39 for helpful details.)

Signing up on the Directory: it costs nothing, commits you to nothing, won't force you into any sort of partnership with anyone—there really are no strings attached. It simply provides a place where you can say 'Our Messy Church welcomes new families and visitors and this is how you get in touch with us.' BRF finds it useful to have as many Messy Churches registered as possible as it gives us an idea of how big we are growing and we can then get in touch to let you know of any developments that can resource you. We also have requests from various sources and countries asking about Messy Churches to visit, and about Messy Churches of different denominations or in different areas, and it's good for our morale to feel less than totally ignorant when we reply!

Messy Meet-ups are organised locally either by Regional Coordinators or by interested individuals. These are simply a gathering of Messy Church team members to chew the fat, swap ideas, weep on shoulders and be energised for the months ahead. Most are advertised on the Messy website diary.

Bigger gatherings: keep an eye open for Messy Weekends and other events organised by BRF to encourage and equip your team before weariness sets in.

Messy Champions gives you or your church the opportunity to share the ministry of BRF's Messy Church by contributing money towards the costs, and prayer towards guiding us in the right direction and to uphold the team. All Messy Champions receive an annual newsletter full of stories of what your gift is helping to happen. You can find the details on the website.

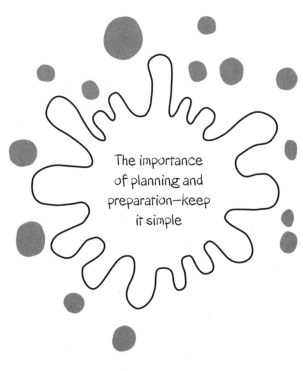

The importance of planning and preparation—keep it simple

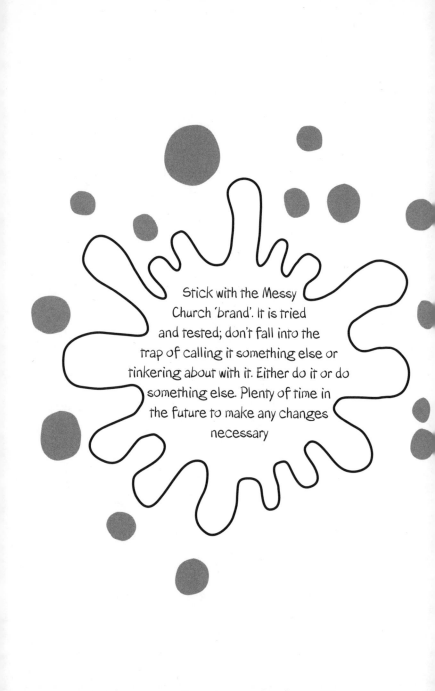

Stick with the Messy
Church 'brand'. It is tried
and tested; don't fall into the
trap of calling it something else or
tinkering about with it. Either do it or do
something else. Plenty of time in
the future to make any changes
necessary

Questions to ask when visiting a Messy Church

Take a deep breath and enjoy the whole experience! Each Messy Church has its own wonderful characteristics but hopefully you'll find the same core values running through each one you visit. And don't panic if things are not what you expect! Sue in Wigan says: 'Two churches sent folk to see what we are doing in our Messy Church but were put off exploring further when they saw the huge numbers (190) attending. They decided they just couldn't cope with so many!'

Remember the Mess you've visited is not *your* church, that there are plenty of equally valid different ways of doing Messy Church and God is there in all of them.

Some suggestions for a visit:

- Let the Messy Church know you are coming so someone can find time to chat with you and show you around.
- If you are travelling by car invite others from your church to travel with you. Who knows what inspiration each person may receive!
- Try to stay for the whole time, as Messy Church invites you to worship with them from the moment you enter until the moment you depart. It's tempting to leave before the meal, but it will give you huge insights if you stay.
- Take a notebook and pen, and a camera to record non-people ideas like instruction sheets or welcome tables (and film only with permission, of course).
- Get contact details from people you talk to. If they are busy you may need to follow up with questions after the visit.

Some suggestions for questions:

- Why did you start a Messy Church?
- Who do you want to come to your Messy Church?
- How did you come to choose this time and day?
- How did you advertise?
- How big is your team?
- Is everyone CRB cleared?
- Is there one main coordinator or more?
- How often do you meet to plan?
- How are you funding your Messy Church?
- How much does it cost to put on one Messy Church?
- From where did you purchase your banner?
- Do you register all ages as they arrive?
- How does everyone know what to do when visiting for the first time?
- How many crafts and activities do you put on each time?
- Where did you find the crafts and activities ideas?
- Do you find the adults enjoy crafts too?
- How do the cooks know how many to cook for?
- Do you have favourite recipes to share?
- Who delivers the Celebration Time?
- Where do you get the songs from?

- Do you take photographs?
- Do you keep a Messy Church Family List of contact details?
- Have you given out any questionnaires?
- Do you offer anything messy mid month?
- What time do you get home after tidying up?
- What do you personally get out of it?

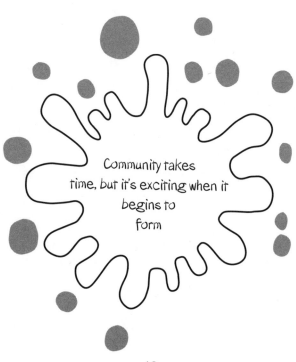

Community takes time, but it's exciting when it begins to form

What to expect

One glorious story tells of a Messy Church starting in a Grade 1 listed church to a congregation with no children on a Sunday. They decided that if their first session brought in 30 people they would be delighted. When numbers hit 70 and still people were coming in, the harassed kitchen team bellowed 'No more! No more! Close the doors!'

Other Messy Churches start with high numbers then find numbers dropping off after a while, or start smaller than they'd hoped and stay small for some time. There is no guarantee that your shepherd's pies will be an ample sufficiency for the three people who turn up or that you'll be praying for a miraculous multiplication of mince to feed the teeming hordes: every Messy Church is different.

When 'too many' turn up, it's worth bracing yourselves to cope without saying no to anyone for a pilot period and seeing whether numbers settle down to something manageable by the end of that time. Obviously if numbers are too high for safety, you'll have to turn people away or find an overflow venue, and if there are too many to cope with, you'll need to consider pleading with members of another local church to run one on a different day, or to join you and help out, or run a parallel one yourselves with a separate team on a different day.

Some people get excited about numbers; others see them as irrelevant. Perhaps it's worth saying that small numbers mean there is a huge opportunity to build strong intimate relationships relatively quickly, to visit effectively and to keep everyone informed; whereas large numbers mean there is a great buzz, little danger of becoming a clique and it's obvious to everyone that there is some measure of success. Big or small, it's a win-win situation.

What else to expect? Some of the following:

- Unlikely people may be your best team members.
- It may take a long time for people to 'warm up' spiritually.
- Unless you work hard at being all-age you'll find yourselves gearing everything towards the children.
- You will get more out of it than you put into it.
- Messy problems may need messy solutions.
- People from Sunday church may keep on expecting Messy families to come to Sunday church.
- God will work in ways you hadn't been expecting.

Organising your team

There is no one best way of organising your team. As you will have gathered, all Messy Churches are different. Here are some approaches that different churches have tried:

- Do it all yourself. This will almost inevitably result in burnout within a few months. Do not do it all yourself!

- Have a core team of two to four easy, competent, hassle-free people to work with and do all the planning and preparation with them. Let the rest of the team simply join you on the day.

- Have a leader responsible for each section of Messy Church and meet with them to get the overall picture, then leave them to organise their own areas of responsibility. You might have a welcome leader, a craft leader, a kitchen leader, a celebration leader and a discipleship leader, each of whom assembles a team of helpers. Planning meetings then simply involve the big picture rather than details.

- Treat the need for a large team as an opportunity to grow disciples and build a team from people who are not yet committed Christians, training them as you go along.

- Insist that the whole of your church comes on board with some form of commitment before you can start.
- Work with another church. If you have a team but a dank mould-ridden vault of a church, they may have a smashing building but no-one who can simultaneously manoeuvre tables, chairs and a Zimmer frame.

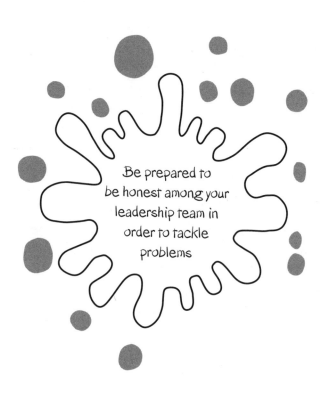

Be prepared to be honest among your leadership team in order to tackle problems

Sustaining your Messy Church and your team

There will be exciting positive months when everything goes well, crowds are pawing at the door asking searching questions about the place of suffering in the world and when every craft leads young and old into a deep relationship with God and with each other. And there will be months where nobody comes except your own family, half the cooks waltz off to Corfu without telling you, the heating breaks down, your own children declare they would rather watch *The X Factor*, the celebration team chooses a song from *Favourite Victorian Sickly Selections*, the crafts appear futile and you get marbling ink all over your favourite top. Things that you can put in place before such a month to help you refrain from hiding under the duvet till it all goes away include:

- Know you are part of the network of people who want to support you (see above 'Why the network?', page 33).
- Establish a regular training/reflection time for your team. The Messy Church DVD has lots of material to help you look at the bigger picture.

- Tell God your frustrations and ask a prayer team to commit to praying for you all every month.
- Remember that God isn't limited by mistakes, and that his strength is made perfect in our weakness: he can and does redeem dire situations.
- Keep a record of 'God-moments'.
- Remind yourself of the bigger picture, of the way you are making disciples, and that this is slow faithful work, not a quick fix, especially among those who have been hurt by church in the past or whose family lives are remarkably messy.
- Think imaginatively about how to grow those disciples you're making: what is the next step for that one person you've noticed is interested?

Evaluation questions after your pilot period

These are suggestions to adapt to your own situation:

Questions to ask the team

- Is our Messy Church sufficiently focused on the needs of people in our own area?
- Is our welcome effective?
- Do we provide activities for all ages and all learning styles?
- Do the craft activities provide links to the theme?
- Is the celebration accessible and relevant to all ages and learning abilities?
- Do we provide opportunities to meet Jesus in every stage of Messy Church?
- Is the team confident to share God's story and their own story?
- Is anyone in the team finding Messy Church too heavy a burden?
- Is everyone safe?
- Are we making disciples?

Questions to ask the congregation

(Perhaps with smiley, sad or neutral faces to circle, and space to add comments.)

How welcome does everyone in your family or group feel?

How do you all find the crafts?

How do you all find the celebration?

How do you all find the meal?

How accessible is the venue?

How is the time and day for you?

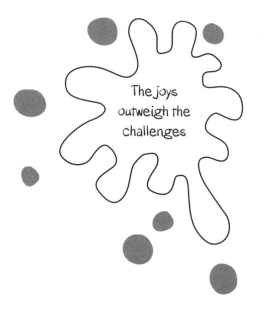

The joys outweigh the challenges

Be encouraged

God is doing something exciting through people like you. A recent email thanked us for what we're doing and added, 'Messy Church is changing the landscape of outreach and worship in big, big ways.' We don't know where this messy journey will take us, but we do know that the more prayer, discernment and integrity goes into starting and sustaining Messy Churches, the more chance we have of catching the wind of the Spirit for our communities in this generation.

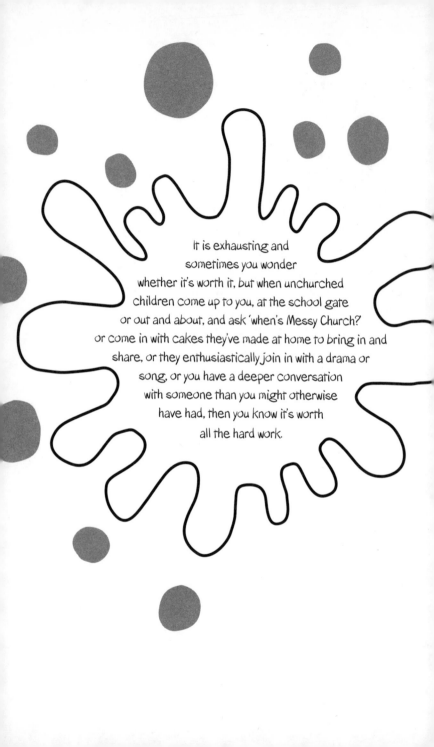

It is exhausting and
sometimes you wonder
whether it's worth it, but when unchurched
children come up to you, at the school gate
or out and about, and ask 'when's Messy Church?'
or come in with cakes they've made at home to bring in and
share, or they enthusiastically join in with a drama or
song, or you have a deeper conversation
with someone than you might otherwise
have had, then you know it's worth
all the hard work.

Registration form

Name of family members at Messy Church
(and d.o.b. optional—for birthday celebrations)

1 _____   _____

2 _____   _____

3 _____   _____

4 _____   _____

5 _____   _____

6 _____   _____

Address _____

_____ Postcode _____

Email _____

Phone _____

Mobile _____

I am interested in belonging to the Messy Church
Facebook page for this church   YES / NO

I would like to be kept informed about Messy Church
by email / text / other (please delete as necessary)

I would rather you didn't contact me about Messy Church yet   ❑

I give permission for photos of me and/or my children taken at Messy Church
by our official photographer to be used for this church's publicity (for example,
during Messy Church on a Powerpoint, in the church magazine/newsletter, or on
the church website). I am aware that this church will always ensure the pictures are
respectful in their nature and appropriate to the activity promoted, and that no
link can be made between the image of my child and his/her full name, address,
email, etc. in order to avoid personal information being displayed or accessed
publicly.

Signed _____ Date _____

About the authors

Lucy Moore works for BRF as Messy Church Team Leader. She is responsible for developing the work of Messy Church nationally and internationally— writing, speaking, reflecting and developing Messy projects. She continues to help lead Messy Church in her own church, where her husband is the minister.

Before working full-time with Messy Church, Lucy was a member of BRF's Barnabas children's ministry team, offering training for those wanting to bring the Bible to life for children in churches and schools across the UK, and using drama and storytelling to explore the Bible with children herself.

Jane Leadbetter is part of the BRF Messy Church Team. She has worked as a primary school teacher and was Children's Work Adviser in the Diocese of Liverpool for twelve years. She now works from home and runs L19: Messy Church once a month on a Saturday, as well as a Beaver Scout Colony and St Mary's Grassendale Tots Team. She is passionate about helping all ages worship together.

Other Messy Church® resources

Messy Crafts

A craft-based journal for Messy Church members

Lucy Moore

This book is a craft book with a difference! As well as bulging with craft ideas to inspire your creativity at Messy Church, it is also a journal to scribble in, doodle on and generally make your own.

The intention is that it will become a scrapbook of conversations, messy moments and prayers—a part of everyday life at home where you can sketch in your own ideas, list useful websites, make notes, reflect on spiritual moments, and journal your Messy Church journey.

ISBN 978 0 85746 068 4 £6.99

Available from your local Christian bookshop or direct from BRF: visit www.brfonline.org.uk

Messy Cooks

A handbook for Messy Church catering teams

Jane Butcher

This book is a handbook for everyone involved in Messy Church catering teams! As well as being a useful treasure store of practical and easy-to-prepare recipes for all your Messy Church events, it also provides tips on quantities, basic cooking skills, essential equipment and ideas for relating food to a Bible story, theme or festival.

There are 36 recipes in total—two delicious main courses and a scrummy dessert for every month of the year. Each recipe includes at least one helpful hint, suggested variations to ring the changes or provide a vegetarian option, and space for you to jot down your own personal reflections, comments and notes.

All the recipes have been used in real Messy Churches, tried and tested in real Messy Church kitchens by real Messy cooks, and enjoyed by real Messy Church families. One Messy cook summed it up by saying, 'We love seeing the children's faces when they come in and ask us, "What's for dinner?"'

ISBN 978 0 85746 069 1   £5.99

Available from your local Christian bookshop or direct from BRF: visit www.brfonline.org.uk

Messy Church®

Fresh ideas for building a Christ-centred community

Lucy Moore

Messy Church is bursting with easy-to-do ideas to draw people of all ages together and help them to experience what it means to be part of a Christian community outside of Sunday worship.

At its heart, *Messy Church* aims to create the opportunity for parents, carers and children to enjoy expressing their creativity, sit down together to eat a meal, experience worship and have fun within a church context.

The book sets out the theory and practice of Messy Church and offers 15 themed programme ideas to get you started, each including:

- Bible references and background information
- Suggestions for ten easy-to-do creative art and craft activities
- Easy-to-prepare everyday recipes
- Family-friendly worship outlines

ISBN 978 1 84101 503 3   £8.99

Available from your local Christian bookshop or direct from BRF: visit www.brfonline.org.uk

Messy Church® 2

Ideas for discipling a Christ-centred community

Lucy Moore

Messy Church is growing! Since it began in 2004, many churches have picked up the idea of drawing people of all ages together and inviting them to experience fun-filled Christian community outside Sunday worship.

Following the popular Messy Church formula, *Messy Church 2* not only provides a further 15 exciting themed sessions, but also explores ways to help adults and children alike to go further and deeper with God—in other words, to grow as disciples.

As before, the material is overflowing with ideas for creativity, fun, food, fellowship and family-friendly worship, but new to *Messy Church 2* are 'take-away' ideas to help people think about their Messy Church experience between the monthly events.

Across the year, the 15 themes explore:

- Loving God, our neighbours and our world
- The life of Jesus: growing up
- Bible women: Ruth, Hannah and Esther
- Christian basics: who God is
- Baptism: belonging to the family of God
- Holy Communion: sharing and caring together

ISBN 978 1 84101 602 3   £8.99

Available from your local Christian bookshop or direct from BRF: visit www.brfonline.org.uk.

Messy Church®—the DVD

Presented by Lucy Moore

Bringing the Messy Church story to life, the DVD is a resource to help those who are thinking of starting a Messy Church to catch the vision, and, for teams already leading a Messy Church, to help develop good practice and inspire further thinking. It features Messy Churches from a variety of situations across the UK, with parents, children, teens and leaders sharing their experiences and wisdom.

The DVD can be used to:

- Introduce the concept of Messy Church
- Help a new team understand what starting a Messy Church might entail
- Help an existing team think through some of the important issues faced by leadership teams as the Messy work goes on

ISBN 978 1 84101 849 2   £9.99

For further resources to help you make best use of the DVD, visit www.messychurch.org.uk/dvd.

Sports Fun for Messy Churches

Lucy Moore

Sports Fun for Messy Churches is a great way to enhance your Messy Church experience by providing fun-filled games and sports activities for families to enjoy together. This book provides a wealth of simple, interactive games and family-friendly sports ideas for Messy Church leaders to use in their sessions. The ideas also pick up a range of healthy living themes.

'Brimming with original, inspirational and fun ideas which will make bodies move, hearts pump and spirits soar. Messy Church and sport is truly a match made in heaven.'

Mark Chester, Family Officer, Liverpool Football Club

ISBN 978 1 84101 824 9   £5.99

Messy Readings

14 messy moments to get you into the Bible

Lucy Moore

There are lots of people belonging to Messy Churches who are starting to see that there may be more to the Bible than they'd thought. This colour booklet of readings taken from our New Daylight Bible reading notes gives everyone a chance to enjoy God's word and see the difference he can make in their lives.

ISBN 978 0 85746 008 0   £1.00

Available from your local Christian bookshop or direct from BRF: visit www.brfonline.org.uk.

Enjoyed

this book?

Write a review—we'd love to hear what you think.
Email: reviews@brf.org.uk

Keep up to date—receive details of our new books as they happen.
Sign up for email news and select your interest groups at:
www.brfonline.org.uk/findoutmore/

Follow us on Twitter @brfonline

By post—to receive new title information by post (UK only), complete the form below and post to: BRF Mailing Lists, 15 The Chambers, Vineyard, Abingdon, Oxfordshire, OX14 3FE

Your Details
Name _____
Address_____
_____
Town/City _____ Post Code _____
Email_____

Your Interest Groups (*Please tick as appropriate)	
❏ Advent/Lent	❏ Messy Church
❏ Bible Reading & Study	❏ Pastoral
❏ Children's Books	❏ Prayer & Spirituality
❏ Discipleship	❏ Resources for Children's Church
❏ Leadership	❏ Resources for Schools

Support your local bookshop
Ask about their new title information schemes.